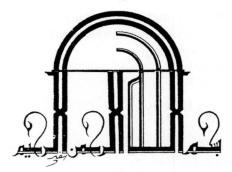

IN THE NAME OF ALLAAH, THE BENEFICIENT, THE MOST MERCIFUL

© Dar Al Taqwa Ltd. 1994

Reprinted 1998
Reprinted 2010

ISBN 1 870582 070

Translation: Aisha Bewley

Editorial: Abdalhaqq Bewley

Published by:
Dar Al Taqwa Ltd.
7A, Melcombe Street
Baker Street
London
NW16AE
web: http://www.daraltaqwaonline.com
email: info@ daraltaqwaonline.com

Printed and Bound by Imak Ofset Printing Center, Istanbul
web: www.imakofset.com.tr
email: isa@imakofset.com.tr

Fate and Predestination

Sheikh Mohammad M.
Al-Sha'rawi

Table of Contents

Chapter One:
The Will of Allah: Sovereign Doer of Whatever He Wills

No question is as controversial as that of Fate and Predestination. You will find that almost every human being wishes to discuss it, whether they have any knowledge about it or not. They ask questions like: "If everything is already written and decreed, why then are we held accountable?" or: "Is it possible for someone to do something that Allah has not decreed?" or: "If this is so, then how can Allah punish me with Hellfire? or: "If I cannot do anything except what has been decreed by Allah, is it fair to be held to account in the Hereafter?"

Such questions are only repeated by those who have wronged themselves and those who are disobedient to Allah. No one ever says the reverse: "If everything is decreed, why then does Allah admit anyone into Paradise to be blessed?" You never hear that question. You only hear: "Being held to account is not fair since everything is decreed by the Will of Allah." In fact, Allah has given man freedom of choice as long as he is alive and this is how the question comes to arise, for the free will granted to man does not, as some people think, conflict with the will of Allah in the phenomenal world. The truth is quite the contrary.

Some people even quote these verses from the Qur'an:

> "*But you will not will unless Allah wills. Indeed Allah is All-knowing, All-wise.*" (76:30)

Addressing His Prophet, may Allah bless him and grant him peace, Allah says:

"You cannot guide those you love; rather Allah guides those He wills." (28:56)

Allah Almighty also says:

"Allah leads astray anyone He wills and guides anyone He wills." (35:7)

Given these verses concerning the will of Allah, why then are we held accountable on the Day of Judgement? The answer is that Allah Almighty only has what He wills in His creation. There is nothing outside this will. Given this fact at the outset, there are, in spite of this, people who let their own hands contribute to their own destruction. Creatures of Allah do things that incur Allah's punishment or His mercy, as Allah says:

"Allah certainly does not wrong people in any way. Rather it is people who wrong themselves." (10:44)

The Universe and Free Will

From the beginning, Allah Almighty created His universe on the basis of freedom of choice. There are those who chose subjugation and those who chose freedom of choice. The choice was available for each group for the period of the time they were to be alive in this existence. There are the angels, the manner of whose creation Allah has veiled from us, and they extol Allah's limitless glory by day and night, and do not disobey Him in anything He commands them to do. The Qur'an testifies to this:

"They glorify by night and by day, never flagging." (21:20)

and also:

"They do not disobey Allah in anything He commands them and they do as they are commanded." (66:6)

The angels are entrusted with Allah's will in the Universe, just as everything in the universe is entrusted to an angel according to the will of Allah. There are the Throne-bearers, the Angels brought near to Allah, the High Angels, the Angels of Death, the angels who are the noble guardians of human beings, those who write down all men's deeds, and so on.

All the different forms of existence in the universe are in submission, for they have chosen to be so. Only men and jinn are not. Look at this verse from the Qur'an:

"We offered the Trust to the heavens and the earth and the mountains and they refused to take it on and were very wary of it. And man took it on. He is indeed wrongdoing and ignorant." (33:72)

From this we know that the heavens, the earth, the mountains and other creatures were offered this Trust or, in other words, freedom of choice. This means that they did have their own choice of whether to be obedient or disobedient. However, all the beings in the universe except man refused free will. They said, "O Lord, we are unable to control ourselves. We are unable to shoulder that trust. Therefore, O Lord, give us submission."

If Allah had not told us about this in the Qur'an, we would not have had the least knowledge that the heavens, the earth, the mountains and other creatures of Allah were offered free will but that they preferred to be subjugated and refused to bear the responsibility of freedom of choice, in contradistinction to man, who accepted that responsibility.

What is that Trust? A trust is when someone entrusts you with something on condition that you give it back when he demands it, when there is no written document or any witness to prove that he has given you that thing. For example, if a person gives you a thousand pounds and takes a receipt or a cheque or an I.O.U. for it, that is not considered to be a trust, but a witnessed deposit. When

3

this takes place between you and that person without any witness or evidence, then it is a trust. When Allah offered that Trust to the heavens, the earth and the mountains, they refused it. Why? Because they felt they would be unable to give it back. When somebody deposits a sum of money with you, it can happen that in the face of some difficulty that occurs you take some of it hoping to replace it. You may even spend the entire amount, believing you will be able to pay it back. Then when you are asked to do so, you may not find the money to pay it back. In that case you have betrayed the trust.

Man accepted the Trust. He imagined he would be able to bear the responsibility and follow the way of Allah: fulfil the rights of Allah over him in respect of prayers, thankfulness, worship and other duties. When man started carrying the Trust, which is life itself, Satan tempted him to commit sin. So he made others co-partners with Allah. He worshipped stones, the sun, the moon, the stars, animals and other things, and then that Trust was betrayed. When death approaches and the time comes for repayment, he meets Allah and is unable to render back His Trust.

Man and the Trust

It was man's choice to bear the Trust, but did he take it on against Allah's will? Did man give himself the free will to act or not to act, or was it given to him by Allah Almighty? Of course, man did not give himself anything. It is Allah - glory be to Him! - who gave that freedom of choice to man and created him with that free will. Had Allah willed to create man as a subjected creature without any choice, He would have done so. For that reason, Allah draws our attention to this fact when He says:

"If We willed We could send down a sign from heaven to them, and then their necks would be lowered to it in subjection." (26:4)

4

And He says:

*"Do those who believe not know that if Allah had willed
He could have guided all mankind?"* (13:31)

In other words, no one is able do anything in the Universe without Allah willing it. Those beings who have chosen submission, only chose it by the will of Allah. Thus everything in existence is subject to the will of its Creator. Those obliged to worship Him were obliged by the will of Allah. Those with the choice of disobeying Him have that choice by the will of Allah. Neither is outside His will. Thus man was created with free will because Allah willed him to have it. Allah's justice forbore from forcing man to choose choice. Rather freedom of choice was offered to man and he accepted it. And the offer came by the will of Allah.

The question here then is: why was man created possessing a free will? We say that all the submitted creatures of Allah affirm His majesty and supremacy. He is All-Able to compel anyone He wills to do anything He wills. There is, however, love for Allah in His universe, which can only be realised by those who willingly and lovingly worship Him - not out of compulsion, but out of love for Him. They worship Him because of their love for Him and obey Him because they love His obedience. This could not occur unless these creatures had full freedom to believe or not to believe, and to obey or disobey.

These creatures are able to say, "O Lord, we love you and therefore we believe in You, not because we are forced to, but out of love. Lord, we love obedience, so we obey You without compulsion and out of love. We will carry out Your commands and avoid Your prohibitions. O Lord, though we are able to commit sins, tempted by our passion and by shaytans among men and jinn, yet, O Lord, our love for You is much greater than our love for the whole world. All that You want us to do, we love to do, for we love You and love what pleases You."

This is the meaning of freedom of choice in the universe. Allah - glory be to Him! - does not need a hollow form of submission, what He wants is humble hearts. He wants man to come to Him

5

with the heart of a lover, for belief is a test of love of Allah in the heart. The greater your love for Him, the greater your belief in His Way. But if your love for Him is weak, you will go far away from His Way.

Allah's Distinguishing of Mankind

In the process of creating man - that creature who would worship Him out of love - Allah Almighty wanted to make him master of this universe as a reward for his obedience. He also wanted to prepare man for the difficult trial he would face during his lifetime, since it requires power and strength on the part of man to resist passion, the whisperings of Satan and all the allurements of sin.

So Allah granted him mastery over things: a universe at his disposal, full of things that keep him alive: a sun that gives him warmth and light during the day so that he is able to develop life in the universe as Allah commanded him; an earth that provides plenty of food for him so that he has a variety of choice, making him free to choose from its produce whatever he likes; varied vegetables and fruits with different flavours; animals providing meat for food and wool for clothing; water falling from the sky to preserve his own life and the life of other things - animals and plants - all at his service. In this way, Allah Almighty has granted man a universe with all that he needs for his livelihood, so that he does not have to busy himself with these needs to the neglect of the Giver of Life.

This is the first distinguishing characteristic which Allah has granted man who possesses free choice. The second distinguishing characteristic is that Allah has given man mastery over all the things that provide him with his basic needs. In other words, those things cannot refuse to perform their duty in existence. The sun cannot say, "I shall rise today but not tomorrow." The moon cannot leave the sky and disappear all of a sudden. The air cannot escape from the earth and deny man life. The earth cannot say, "I will not produce any plants." Therefore everything in the universe is at the service of man and performs its task in a perfect way.

This subjected universe is a suitable and stable one, for it does not tire anyone or spoil anything. Its laws are perfect, constant and carried out by the command of Allah. This is done so that man need not worry about his continued existence and survival. He is not worried about whether the sun will rise in time. He is not busy looking for a way to make water fall from the sky. He is not responsible for making day and night succeed one another. He is not searching for a means to protect the atmosphere which surrounds earth. Allah has relieved him from all these cares so that he would not become so concerned for the universe that he forgets about its Creator.

Clear Signs for Mankind

Then comes the third distinguishing human characteristic. Allah wanted man to know that there is only one All-Powerful God, Who has created all these things for his service and that this God is the same God Who created man and this universe. He has made things which are much stronger than man, and which no one could lay claim to making, to be at the service of man. The sun gives off light and heat without burning up the whole universe. Man cannot ward off its harm. Not even humanity in its entirety can claim to have made or created the sun, with its power and strength.

Allah - glory be to Him! - made the sun to provide for our needs while with His wisdom, knowledge and perfect craftsmanship He simultaneously made it harmless. The seas, likewise, could flood the whole world, but Allah Almighty has made them provide all kinds of fish. The sea provides us with food and ornaments such as pearls and coral. He has made it carry our ships from one country to another and has made it harmless. The earth is also potentially able to shake violently and destroy man and all that he has built, but Allah has subdued it and made it firm and stable for us to live on.

Then Allah - glory be to Him - has granted us a fourth distinguishing characteristic: ears with which to hear, eyes with which to see, a tongue with which to talk, all the senses necessary to know what is around us, and an intellect in order to be able to discriminate.

All these things that serve us cannot be made by any human being. We must therefore realise that there is a tremendous power which has created this universe and subjected it to us, and that this Power is beyond and above any other power. Concerning this Allah Almighty says:

"Allah brought you out of your mothers' wombs knowing nothing at all, and gave you hearing and sight and hearts so that hopefully you might be thankful." (16:78)

These clear and evident signs have been created by Allah to demonstrate that He is the Creator, so that the human intellect would not become exhausted in its search to reach Him. Allah has not made these signs vague or hidden or unattainable. He has granted man sight to see them and witness them without any trouble. We see the sun, the moon, the stars, plants, the earth. We breathe the air and see the signs of Allah which attract our attention in order to proclaim both themselves and their Creator without too much effort on our part.

Allah Almighty has commanded us to look at the universe and see these signs in order not to become preoccupied and lose ourselves in the attempt to look for His cosmic signs; in other words, so that we will not preoccupy ourselves with creatures to the extent of forgetting the Creator. As a general rule, the human mind, even without any education, is easily able to see these signs and recognise them. In this way, Allah has willed us to busy ourselves with Him and our love for Him without becoming lost looking for indistinct signs in His universe.

Man and Shaytan

Then comes the fifth distinguishing human trait. Before we started our free will phase, Allah Almighty wanted to teach us that we were going to be tempted by Satan, and further that this temptation is a lie, and that Satan is our enemy, trying to deceive us with false hopes which will never be fulfilled. He whispers to us his lies which are without basis, and tries hard to drive us away from our love of Allah and our obedience to Him. The temptation of Adam and Eve was a trial. Allah settled them in Paradise and allowed them to eat from all its fruits except one, exactly as He has permitted us to enjoy plenty of things and has prohibited us very few.

In Paradise, Adam and Eve were allowed to eat from all the fruits except one tree. Satan came to tempt them to eat from that one tree. He lied to them saying that the fruits of this tree would make them immortal and would give them an everlasting kingdom. He swore to them, but it was a lie. Adam and Eve believed him and they ate of the tree, which instead of giving them immortality, revealed their nakedness and shame. Instead of giving them everlasting wealth, it deprived them of Allah's sustenance which they had received without the least work or effort. They descended to the earth having to work and toil and suffer in order to make a living. This was the beginning of life on earth, and demonstrated Satan's part in it with the false hopes that he holds out to man in order to drive him into sin.

To stop man being overcome by his fear of Satan, Allah Almighty told him that Satan's cunning is in fact very weak. This means he cannot overcome man until the latter is willing to obey him. Allah also told us that Satan has no power to force us to do something we do not want to do. Allah has neither given him the power to compel us to disobey nor the persuasive ability to coerce us into committing a sin. The Qur'an tells us that Satan will say to us:

"I had no authority over you." (14:22)

This means that Satan has in reality no power to force us to commit sin or tempt us to do it. Then Allah Almighty wanted us to rest assured that if we sincerely worship Him and truly love Him, He - glory be to Him! - will be sufficient defender against the evil of Satan. He says in the Qur'an:

> *"He [Iblis] said, 'My Lord, because of the way You misguided me, I will make things on the earth seem attractive to them and will misguide them all, every one of them, except Your slaves among them who are truly sincere.' He said, 'This is a straight path towards Me. You have no authority over any of My slaves except for the misguided who follow you.'"* (15:39-42)

Thus Allah - glory be to Him! - wants to tell us that Satan's whisperings will be unable to affect any who are devoted and sincere in their love and worship of Him. But when the human self becomes weak, then Allah has told us to seek refuge with Him. Then the suggestions of Satan will be removed by Him. In this situation, He says that you should say:

> *"Say: 'O Lord, I seek refuge with You from the goadings of the Shaytans, and I seek refuge with You, O Lord, from their being present with me.'"* (23:97-98)

And He also says:

> *"Those who are Godfearing, when they are bothered by a visitation from Shaytan, remember, and immediately see clearly."* (7:201)

In this way Allah shows us the way to defeat Satan. All we have to do is to seek refuge with Him and be sincere in our worship of Him, thus preventing Satan's cunning from paralysing us.

Our testifying to His Lordship

The sixth distinguishing characteristic came when Allah made us testify to His Lordship while we were still in the form of spirits known only to Him. In this way, He created innate faith in our hearts so that we would have a natural disposition towards belief in Allah the Greatest Creator. This testimony was made so that we would have no argument on the Day of Judgement, for man is overly inclined to argument. That is why when the name of Allah is mentioned, we find it familiar and recognisable, even though Allah cannot be seen by us. It is this innate nature - that inclination towards belief which Allah equipped us with before we came to this life to start our experience of freedom of choice - which we accepted by His will. Allah says:

> *"When your Lord took out from the loins of the children of Adam all their descendants and made them bear witness against themselves: 'Am I not your Lord?' They said, "We bear witness that indeed You are!' Lest you say on the Day of Rising, 'We were unmindful of this.' Or lest you say, 'Our forefathers associated others with Allah before, and we are merely descendants coming after them. Are You then going to destroy us for what those falsifiers did?'"* (7:172-173)

Up to this point, we have indicated that we were created with freedom of choice by the will of Allah, and we accepted it. Our being created with free will is entirely in harmony with this verse:

> *"But you shall not will unless Allah wills. Surely Allah is All-Knowing, All-Wise."* (76:30)

Allah has willed us to have freedom of choice and our choice springs from His will. He has set up guarantees of our freedom to choose in His creation of the universe and His signs in the universe and in the journey of life itself. Therefore nothing should divert us from worshipping Him, that being the purpose for which

11

He created us, nor from our love for Him who created this life for us. When Allah sent Messengers to show us the perfect path to follow, it was because He loved us. He did want not to make our search for knowledge of our Creator, who wants us to do certain particular things, difficult for us. The Messengers came to tell us that the Creator and Fashioner is Allah who wants us to worship and love Him. They came with a simple, clear system put into practice by the Prophets in front of Allah's servants. Thus Allah has saved us from mental confusion in our search for the Creator and what He wants us to do. However human free will is not absolute. It is limited in the path of Allah to what we can and cannot do.

Chapter Two:
Man's Free Will

Man was created with free will, but has Allah given man absolute freedom of choice? Some shallow liberals, who claim that they are free and follow their reason and ideals, enthusiastically say, "Yes, we have absolute freedom of choice." Some have even gone further and stated that an intelligent man is able to make his own destiny and can put himself in whatever position he likes in this life.

To all these we say: "Do not go so fast, for what you say is completely unjustified and life and all its events belie it. Allah - glory be to Him! - did not give man unlimited choice; He gave him a choice that is appropriate for his function in existence. As Allah is the All-Wise, He necessarily acts with wisdom. And because He is the All-Knowing, everything in His universe is done with knowledge. Nothing is chaotic or haphazard or happens without coherence. The fact is that man was not granted absolute free will."

If someone attempts to review his life, or rather looks deeply into himself or into the working of his body, he will discover that there are many things which are beyond his freedom to choose. The truth is that most of man's life is not subject to his own choice.

Let us start from the very beginning, when man comes into the world in the first moments of his life, when the first air goes into his lungs at the time of his birth. Does he choose the place of his birth? Does he choose the day of his birth and the hour of his birth? No, none of us chooses the moment of his coming into the world. In other words, we all come into this life by the will of Allah - glory be to Him! Consequently the beginning of every human being, the place of that beginning, their sex, and nationality

- Arab, British or American - are not their choice. Then comes the body: tall or short? The colour of the eyes, the colour of the hair, the facial features; the identity of their father and mother; whether the hearing, sight, and limbs are sound and healthy? In respect of all these and many other things, man is not free to choose. Allah - glory be to Him - draws our attention to man's limited choice from the time of his birth, saying in the Qur'an:

"It is He who forms you in the wombs however He wills." (3:6)

Thus Allah has attributed all that is connected with the moment of birth and the formation of the human being to His absolute Might alone. Man was never given any choice about being born black or white, healthy or sick, nor was he given freedom to choose the features of his face or the shape of his body.

The Limits of Free Will

To those who claim that man was given absolute free will in the universe, we say that your own birth belies you, for the time of man's birth is beyond his own choice.

To complete the picture, we have to move from the time of birth - the moment when man comes into the world - to the time of the death - the moment he leaves it. Does man have any freedom of choice in respect of death? Does he have the power to say, when the time of death comes, "I will not die now," or "I will delay my death until tomorrow or until next year." Of course not, and Allah - glory be to Him! - has drawn our attention to this fact in many verses of the Qur'an. He says:

"Every nation has a fixed term. When their fixed term arrives, they cannot delay it an hour nor can they bring it forward." (7:34)

Concerning those who believe that death is connected to the events of life, such as war or military expeditions, and think that if a man stays at home in safety, death will not come to him, Allah says:

"O you who believe! Do not be like those who reject and say to their brothers, when they travel in the land or go on raids, 'If they had been with us, they would not have died or been killed.'" (3:156)

And He also says:

"Those who say of their brothers, when they themselves had sat back, 'If they had obeyed us, they would not have been killed.' Say, 'Stave off death from yourselves then if you are telling the truth.'" (3:168)

These two great verses tell us about the unbelievers and the hypocrites, and how they made a connection between death on the one hand and human will and cosmic events on the other. In the first verse, the unbelievers tell their brothers that if they had not travelled and endangered their lives or gone to war where they died or were slain, then they would not have died or been slain. They connected the time and place of death with travel and going to war, and made the cause of death an empirical matter. They thought that if those whose time for death had come and who were either to die or be slain had remained at home and not moved, they would have survived. However, death comes by the will of Allah without any cause, for death itself is the cause. When someone dies, it is because his appointed term has come to an end. A soldier may survive many battles, while someone else dies in his bed. Khalid ibn al-Walid died in bed, although he fought a great number of battles. When he was dying he said:

"I took part in such-and-such battles and expeditions. There is no place in my body which does not have a sword wound or scar from an arrow or spear. Now I am forced to die on my bed like an old camel. May the eyes of cowards never taste sleep!"

15

Thus there is no relationship between death and man's participation, or lack of it, in war, for someone might die at home while someone else comes back safe from the battlefield.

In the second verse, Allah, with an argument full of wisdom, answers the hypocrites who did not go out to fight *jihad* and who were talking to their fellow hypocrites. The hypocrites said, "Had the believers obeyed us and not taken part in war, they would have remained alive like us. But Allah answered them, "You did not go to the fight. You stayed behind. When death comes to you, defend yourselves against it if your claim is true."

Of course, no one can withstand death when his appointed time comes, whether he is on the battlefield or hiding at home or in any other place. Allah clarifies this issue in the verses revealed about the Battle of Uhud. When the Muslims were defeated, the hypocrites and the waverers told themselves that if they had had any say in the matter, they would not have gone to the battle or been killed. Allah answered them:

"They say, 'Do we have any part in the affair at all?'
Say, 'The entire affair belongs to Allah.' They are hiding
in themselves things they do not show you, saying, 'If we
had had any part in the affair, none of us would have been
killed here.' Say, 'Even if you had been in your houses,
those whose killing was decreed would have gone out to
their killing-ground.'" (3:154)

This means that the hypocrites concealed this talk of theirs and did not reveal it to the Prophet, may Allah bless him and grant him peace. Allah wanted to expose them and to inform His Prophet, may Allah bless him and grant him peace, of their secret talk, and at the same time to answer them. This answer came from Allah, the Truthful, Who let His Prophet know what was going on in their minds. He asked His Prophet to tell them that their presence on the battlefield would neither have hastened their death nor delayed it. If they had been at home, those whose time for death had come would have gone out to meet their death at the appointed place.

In other words, caution and avoidance of danger do not prolong or increase life expectancy, because this depends on the will of Allah and His decree must take its course. In fact those who are destined to die do their best to reach the place they are to die. For instance you see a man insisting on travelling by air, doing everything he can to get a seat on board a particular flight, when, all the time, his death lies there, for the aeroplane is destined to crash and all those on board will die. You also see someone determined to visit a place, encountering many difficulties on his way, but when he arrives, he finds death waiting for him. Death comes by a decree from Allah and no one can escape it.

The Appointed Time and the Divine Decree

With utmost clarity, Allah - glory be to Him! - explains further when He says:

"What do you think about those who left their homes in thousands in fear of death? Allah said to them, 'Die!' and then brought them back to life." (2:243)

This verse was revealed to tell the story of the people of a certain village which was attacked by a plague. Its people feared death and so they all abandoned the village. Allah - glory be to Him! - wanted to teach them that there is no escape from His decree, and that when He wills them to die, their departure to another place is of no avail. So He caused them to die and then He brought them back to life because of the prayers of their Prophets.

Therefore it is impossible to escape death, as it has a fixed term which cannot be delayed or advanced a single second. Allah has not made the cause and time of death known so that anyone could say that it is a mechanical process, whereby man becomes old and dies; or that there is a fixed duration for the life of each of us and that we are born and then die at the age of sixty or seventy. The Absolute Might of Allah has created death without any discernable cause - a foetus dies in his mother's womb, a sick man dies because of his illness, a healthy man from no apparent cause. Children, young people, old people die. All this takes place by the will of Allah and needs no cause. There may be two patients with the same disease both treated by the same doctor, but one dies in a few days and the other survives for years.

There is one argument concerning death based on someone condemning another to death and then the latter dying, or someone saying, "I can cause death when I use a cannon, a gun, or a knife and then kill whomever I wish to make die," and then the other person dies. In this way some people claim that death can be in the hands of human beings, meaning that when I want someone to die, I murder him and so he dies. We say that this is to confuse death and killing. Allah alone causes death, while man does not cause death, but he can kill. Look at this verse:

"Muhammad is but a Messenger. Messengers have passed away before him. If he dies or is killed, are you going to turn round on your heels?" (3:144)

It can be seen from this death is not the same as manslaughter, since Allah says, *"dies or is killed."* He also differentiates between them in many other verses of the Qur'an. For example:

"If they had been with us, they would not have died or been killed." (3:156)

And also:

"Those who emigrate in the way of Allah and then are killed or die, Allah will provide them with handsome provision." (22:58)

And further:

"If you die or are killed, you will surely be gathered together before Allah." (3:158)

Death and Killing

Death is different from killing. In the case of death, it comes first and then the body is broken up. But in the case of killing, the body is broken first and, as a consequence, death takes place, as happens when someone hits another person and smashes his head, or fires bullets at his heart or head. First, his body is destroyed, and then his soul departs and he dies. But death takes life first, and then the body breaks down. This is caused by Allah and not by man. Killing destroys the body and leaves it lifeless. The king who argued with Ibrahim, peace be upon him, about his Lord concerning life and death was told by Ibrahim:

> *"When Ibrahim said, 'My Lord is He who gives life and makes die,' he said, 'I too give life and make die.'"*
> (2:258)

He was not telling the truth, for life and death are given by Allah, while man is able to kill, but not to give life.

We have encountered, then, two points where man has no free choice, namely life and death. The third is sleep. Sleep is still a miracle which bewilders the entire world. That is because sleep is an undiscovered territory for the whole world. As soon as man closes his eyes, he moves in just a moment from one set of laws to a completely different set. In the state of waking consciousness, man hears with his ears, sees with his eyes, talks with his tongue and walks on his feet. He is limited by space and time, and controlled by well-known laws. He cannot, for example, travel from Egypt to the U.S.A. without it taking several hours and him having to go through specific procedures. He must go to the airport, pass through emigration control, board the plane and spend several hours before he arrives there, and then he has to go through immigration, etc. again on arrival.

While awake, man sees with his eyes according to their power of vision. There are some people whose vision is strong and who can see for long distances, and others with short sight who need spectacles. Sight is sometimes barred by something in front, such as a wall, preventing one from seeing what is behind it. In the waking state man walks on his legs and even if he hurries his speed is limited. In the waking state, man is subject to material laws. If he falls from a great height, he will be killed or his bones will be crushed. There are many things he cannot see, such as people who have passed away, even if he visits their graves. He cannot talk to them. We could continue listing the laws of the waking state known to us *ad infinitum*.

Dreams and the Waking State

The moment man falls asleep, all these laws are annulled. He might find that he has travelled to the United States and back several times in a few minutes. He sees strange things and places he has never seen before. All these he sees with closed eyes, without being able to see or feel someone's finger, however close to his eyes it might be, because his eyes are closed. Meanwhile, in his sleep, he clearly sees unbelievable and incredible things, such as the vision seen by the King of Egypt in the time of Yusuf, peace be upon him. Allah Almighty says:

> *"I dreamt I saw seven fat cows which seven thin ones ate."* (12:43)

Do cow eat cows in real life? Of course not. We have never seen such a thing. Would thin, weak cows devour strong, fat ones? Of course not; it is incredible.

In sleep, people walk while their feet remain motionless in bed. They travel from place to place while their bodies stay put, not moving even an inch. They can see in their sleep those who passed away a long time ago and talk to them. They may see themselves as young when, in reality, they are old, or see themselves fighting with and defeating a lion. All these things and many others may take place during our sleep. We dream them and we see them and they are not outside the limits of our intellects and memories. For when we get up, we are able to narrate exactly what we have seen in our dream. Our memory comprehends what we have seen; otherwise we would not be able to describe it. A faculty of visual perception other than the physical eye saw clearly in elaborate detail; otherwise we should be unable to describe the things we have seen in our sleep. Even the dialogue that takes place with those who have passed away we understand and know, for we can remember and narrate the actual words and phrases uttered.

Thus, in one instant, man can move from one set of laws to others of which we know nothing. But these are laws to which we are subject in our sleep. The question here is: Do we have any free will or choice in our sleep while we are subject to these laws? In other words, has any of us the freedom to choose the incidents he will see in his dream, so that he could say, "I will see this, but not that," or "I will talk to A and not B" or "Tonight I will visit Europe in my dream but in my next dream I will visit Russia"?

Of course not, for when man sleeps he is outside the realm of human choice. He is no longer free to choose what he will see and not see; he is not able to choose to say some things and not say others; and the things he sees are beyond his control even though his dream may be completely logical. When someone tells you that he saw something in a dream, you do not call him a liar or argue with him, because you know that there are such things as dreams and visions during sleep and that you yourself are also subject to them. You do not accuse him of telling you unbelievable things; you simply do not try to apply the laws that pertain to the waking state. Those laws are not the criteria for what takes place in sleep. We should not subject the dreams which someone has to logic or dispute them, for you know from your own experience that it is possible to see things in dreams which are not subject to logic and ordinary laws.

No one has been able to or will be able to explain in a scientific way the laws which control man in his sleep; how he moves from one state to another in a single moment; how he reverts to the laws of the waking state when he wakes up and to the laws of sleep when he falls asleep. No one, however knowledgeable, can specify how this movement from one law to the other takes place.

However, we do know that sleep is a reality experienced by every human being, and we also know that in our sleep we move beyond the limits of time. When Allah - glory be to Him! - put the Companions of the Cave to sleep for three hundred and nine years, they did not realise how long they had slept when they were awakened. Although they had slept for such a long time, what did they say when they woke up? Allah says:

> *"One of them said, 'How long have you been here?'*
> *They said, 'We have been here a day or part of a day.'"*
> (18:19)

Thus man in his sleep is not conscious of time. The Companions of the Cave had been asleep for a period of time in the same way that all men sleep for a period every day. When someone is tired, he might sleep for an entire day, but very rarely more than that. Applying this to ourselves, when we get up from sleep, we do not know the exact amount of hours we have slept unless we look at an device for measuring the time, such as a clock or a watch, or some other sign indicating the time, like daylight or nightfall, since we may have gone to sleep during the day and woken up at night, or vice versa. However, the exact number of hours is only known if we look at the clock.

Laws Beyond our Reach

It was the will of Allah - glory be to Him! - to make us feel at ease without searching for the laws of sleep because we will never be able to grasp them. He says:

> *"Allah takes back all souls at the time of their death*
> *and those which have not yet died during their sleep. He*
> *retains those whose death has been decreed and sends the*
> *others back for a specified term. In that there are certainly*
> *signs for a people who reflect."* (39:42)

Thus we must know that sleep follows the laws of the *Barzakh* (the interspace between this world and the Next) about which we know nothing except what Allah has told us. Therefore we shall never know anything about the laws of sleep except that man is able to see with eyes other than the ordinary ones; that he moves with a power other than the legs which he uses in everyday life; that he speaks with a different tongue from the one he uses in the state of waking consciousness; and that the state of the *Barzakh* does not depend on the senses of the material body, which are superseded by others during sleep. We are equipped with other senses which we use in the *Barzakh,* where human will plays no part, just as it plays no part in the state of sleep. We are not time-conscious in the *Barzakh* or our sleeping states. We see those who passed away before us in both states.

These things are given to us by Allah as mercy to our minds to enable us to grasp the existence of things that are unknown to us, so that we can visualise the coming state of the *Barzakh.* We should also know that the movement from the state of consciousness to that of the *Barzakh* takes place in just an instant, and therefore understand what is meant by the words of the Prophet, may Allah bless him and grant him peace:

"By Allah, surely you will die as you sleep, and you will be resurrected as you wake up."

As a consequence, we must see that man's freedom of choice in this life is not absolute. Rather, it is a limited one. He has no choice about the time and place of his birth or about his parents, sex, country, physique, or the colour of his eyes, and so on. He also has no choice about the length of his life or the time of his death. Likewise he has no volition in his sleep. Thus the zone of choice is already to some extent limited. The more we proceed to define the freedom of choice granted by Allah to His servants the narrower we will see that it becomes.

Chapter Three:
Freedom of Choice and the Body

We have explained the fact that Allah - glory be to Him! - has not given man absolute freedom of choice, but rather a very limited freedom that accords with his existential function, and this also applies to the duties imposed on him by the path of Allah. Now we move to another area, that of the human body, to see whether it belongs to man in such a way that he can do whatever he wishes with it, or whether Allah has willed us to know that the human body in fact belongs to Allah, and has merely been granted to us for a certain period as a trial.

The human body is subjugated to Allah in most respects, in all that is connected to life and its functions and so on. In our bodies, there are many parts we know nothing about. We do not feel them except during illness or injury. So long as they perform their functions normally, we do not feel them.

We shall begin with those parts which are wholly subjugated to Allah, and then move on to those parts which are subjugated to Allah but over which we also exercise a measure of control.

Let us look first at the life cycle in our bodies. We eat food and chew it with our teeth; it goes through the throat to the stomach to be digested in a mechanical and complicated process; then it moves to the small intestines where the nourishing elements are absorbed into the body to provide it with nutrients which are carried by the blood to the various parts of the body, while the waste is expelled from the intestines.

If we begin with the food, do we have anything to do with the internal reactions between body and food? The answer is no, for when food gets down to the stomach and the various enzymes are secreted, it becomes an involuntary process. No one can tell his stomach to produce the necessary enzymes for digestion nor can he stop these enzymes from digesting food. It is an internal process that takes place inside our bodies and we do not feel it. If we watch a film about what takes place inside the stomach after the food is swallowed, we will be amazed at the Divine power which has made all these processes take place in the stomach without our realising it. Many people live and die without ever knowing how their stomach works to digest food or what the glands are that secrete enzymes for digestion.

Next we come to the liver, which has essential functions in the body: do we know what it does and what it does not do? Do we feel when it starts its work or its functions? No, we do not, for the liver works in the body without our knowing or feeling the process inside our bodies. The probability is that, during our entire life, we will not even feel its existence, so long as it functions properly.

Do we know what the small intestines do? Are we able to make the heart beat or stop beating when we want it to? In your lungs, the process of exchanging oxygen and carbon dioxide is going on night and day. Do you affect this exchange? Do you know anything about blood circulation and what it does in your body? The blood is formed of tens of ingredients: red cells, white cells, etc. Do you know anything about it?

There are battles that take place inside the veins. When microbes attack sick bodies, the white cells fight back and prepare all sorts of defences that kill the microbes and bring back health. Do you do that? Of course not.

Therefore, all these processes are directly subject to Allah and you do not know anything about it. When you perceive this, you cannot help but be stunned by all that takes place in your body while you are unaware of it.

Most important of all, you have no will or control over these processes that work inside your body. In other words, these processes do not take any instructions from you. You cannot make them work or stop them working. This is a sign of Allah's mercy, for if these things were subject to your will, it would truly be a great calamity.

Imagine that you had to instruct the heart to beat, the stomach to function, the lungs to breathe. You would not have the time to do all this. Even if you had time, you would not be able to work for a living, promote progress or implement the laws of Allah. Moreover, you would not be able to sleep, for how could you go to sleep if the heart was following your orders? It would stop when you went to sleep. And how could a little child with no knowledge make these systems work continually?

Compulsion and the Body

You are, then, under subjugation, in respect of most of your bodily parts. This coercion is exerted by Allah - glory be to Him! - out of His mercy to you, to enable you to live, work, and strive. If you had freedom of choice in respect of these things, you would not survive.

Thus, most of the human bodily parts are subjected entirely to Allah. They work by compulsion, not by volition. They do what Allah wills them to do, and stop when He commands them to stop.

You have no freedom of choice concerning most of them and know nothing about them except what Allah wills you to know. If He wills to conceal the knowledge of something in the body from human beings, He does so. This may sound strange, but Allah has also hidden the spirit (*ruh*) from His human creatures. He says:

> "They will ask you about the Spirit. Say: 'The Spirit is my Lord's affair. And the amount of knowledge you have been given is very little.'" (17:85)

Where is the Soul?

Let all the scholars of the whole world gather together. They will not be able to say where the soul that gives life to the body is.

Is it in the beating heart? Or is it rather in the reflective intellect? Or in the continually circulating blood. Or in the walking foot or seeing eye or hearing ear? Where is it? Science cannot provide us with an answer to this question, for it is and always will remain secret, known only to Allah, the Truth.

You feel the soul in your body and perceive its traces, for it provides you with life. And yet you know nothing about it: Allah has concealed its secret from you. How can you say that your body is subject to your will? No, it is controlled by its Creator.

Limbs which are subject to the will

Now we move to the things in your body that Allah has subjected to your will. The tongue, for example, is subject to your will, since it obeys you when you wish to testify that there is no god except Allah alone and say it, just as it also obeys you if you wish to utter disbelief. May Allah protect us from that!

Your eye obeys you if you look at *halal* things and to contemplate Allah's cosmic signs. Likewise, it obeys you in looking at prohibited things. The hand obeys you when you wish to help a disabled person to cross the street, just as it obeys you when you want to harm a weak person or kill an enemy. Your feet obey you if you wish to go to the mosque or desire to visit a pub or a brothel.

All these parts obey you when you wish to be obedient and also obey you when you want to commit disobedience. They neither obey nor disobey for they are tools subject to your will. However we must know two important facts. Firstly, all these things glorify Allah. Secondly, Allah created your body from clay and this clay, of which the human body is composed, has chosen to be obedient.

It glorifies Allah of its own volition. It will obey the unbeliever when he wishes to do something, but at the same time, it curses him. On the Day of Judgement, it will testify against him and it will cause him to enter Hellfire. This is the truth from the Qur'an:

"On the day when their tongues and hands and feet bear witness against them about what they were doing." (24:24)

Also we find:

"They will say to their skins, 'Why did you testify against us?' And they will say, 'Allah gave us speech as He has given speech to everything. He created you the first time round and to Him you will be returned." (41:21)

So all the parts of the body that are subjected to your will are only subjected in appearance. In reality they all glorify Allah. On the Day of Judgement, when the unbelievers enter Hellfire, these bodies will feel great joy for they cause him to suffer and feel the punishment as a penalty for his disobedience.

If you wish to make a concrete experiment to confirm this, then look at the people during the *hajj*. You will discover that, although they sleep very little during the night, their bodies, surprisingly, are comparatively unaffected by tiredness and lack of sleep. The people on *hajj* get up from sleep after only one or two hours and can be seen to be very fresh and active. Why is this? The reason is that the body which glorifies Allah gets its rest through all the glorification and prayers and all the deeds and actions of the *hajj*. That is why the body does not need to fall asleep or even doze to the neglect of remembering Allah, His glorification, or prayers to Him except for a few hours. In this state of harmony, a believer never feels tired.

But in the case of the unbeliever who does not perform anything but sin, you find that his body becomes exhausted from disobedience. That is why he sleeps so much and when he wakes up, feels the need for yet more sleep. Because of the sins they abhor, the tired parts of his body need to rest. The only thing that keeps the unbeliever away from sin is sleep. His body becomes exhausted and needs sleep for long periods.

When people go to perform *hajj*, you hear many of them say that they had an extraordinary power while doing the deeds of *hajj* and that they only slept very little, yet even so they felt very active and fresh. They did not feel the need for sleep because they wished to be awake all night and day.

This happens, but few understand the reason - which is that the parts of the human body are in harmony with obedience to its Creator. They desire only very little sleep. This is the reality of belief in its effect on the human body.

You have no choice concerning your body

There are both subjugated parts in your body which are not subject to your choice, and other parts which are subject to your choice. It is Allah who has made them subject to you, not you yourself. It is Allah - glory be to Him! - who has given you that choice and made these parts of your body subject to your orders so that they will testify for and against you on the Day of Reckoning concerning the good deeds you do and the evil deeds you commit.

Allah - glorify be to Him! - wants to attract our attention to this so that we do not think these parts are subject to us of our own volition. If that belief were well-founded, we would be able to see merely by the fact of having eyes. However, there are some people who have two open eyes, but cannot see. If sight were automatic, we would not find people with two eyes who could not see. Allah has created people with two legs but cannot walk, so that we realise that legs do not walk by themselves through the power of the person who owns them, but rather that they walk by the power of Allah. If they had been able to walk by themselves, we would not see people who possess two legs but are unable to walk. Allah has created people who have two ears but are unable to hear. If hearing were automatic, then everyone who had two ears could hear, and whoever had a tongue could speak.

These few examples created by Allah in His universe are there to attract our attention to the fact that our organs are subjected to us by the power of the Creator and not by our own power. He has provided for those who have lost their sight, hearing, or the ability to walk, equipping them with other capacities which give them excellent qualities that more than compensate for their loss.

He has given us examples showing us that such losses are not necessarily impediments hindering people who suffer them from being geniuses. The famous deaf musician, Beethoven, composed the sweetest music, although he was unable to even hear the music he composed. Taha Husayn was a literary genius even though he was blind and unable to read. Allah created many people of genius who were able to excel although they had lost some of their sensory faculties. He wanted us to see these very limited examples as evidence that the abilities in man come not from himself, but from Allah, who has subjected these things to him.

A Very Limited Choice

Thus far we have seen that man's choice in respect of his body is limited to the energy granted him by Allah who put it under man's command. We have also seen that all man can do is to direct this capacity, given by Allah, to the act he wants to do; but is this choice open?

We can safely say that there are many things in this life which are beyond your ability to choose. First of these is the power of Allah. You have no freedom of choice concerning the things which happen to you by Divine Decree, for they are outside the domain of your free will.

If someone is walking in the street and is struck by a car or if a stone hits him or if he catches a disease - do any of these things fall into the domain of his choice? Can he prevent any of these things from happening to him by the power of Allah? Of course he cannot. Can he prevent any disease from affecting his body? Of course not, for none of us can ward off anything that Allah has decreed will befall us and we cannot avoid it.

That is the first thing that limits our domain of choice, since we are all subject to Allah's power in the face of which neither we nor any other person can do anything. So, whatever is said about man's free choice, it exists only within the limits decreed by Allah. You cannot protect yourself or your children against any harm Allah has decreed will befall you. You cannot prevent any benefit Allah has decreed for you from coming to you. This is the same for all of us, whether rich or poor, strong or weak, privileged or underprivileged. In respect of this matter, we have to call attention to these words of Allah - glory be to Him!:

> *"Say, 'O Allah! Owner of the Kingdom! You give the kingdom to anyone You will, You take the kingdom from anyone You will. You exalt anyone You will, You abase anyone You will. All good is in Your hands. You are over all things powerful.'"* (3:26)

When we look at this verse, we know that power comes only from Allah, not from any human planning, and that Allah is the One who is the Creator of all causes and effects in respect of anyone He pleases.

Qadar (Divine Predestination) acts in many ways to establish someone in authority independently of his ability to do it for himself. Every human being wants authority and strives hard for it, but it comes only from the power of Allah - glory be to Him! - for He is the real Possessor of power and authority.

The earth together with all its creatures is owned by Allah and He gives His kingdom to anyone He wishes. If it had been that people get power of their own, they would have kept it without having it taken from them. Allah says of Himself:

> *"All good is in Your hands. You are over all things powerful."* (3:26)

This is proof that power is wrested by force from people, and that they never relinquish it willingly but have it taken from them in spite of themselves.

Thus you may see someone who is at the summit of power, obeyed and submitted to by all. Then, in a moment, the command of Allah comes and even his nearest relations forsake him and he is in fear, trying to save his life or struggling to find some shelter to protect himself. Power and authority are not in his hands, but are only his by the power of Allah - glory be to Him!

The whole question is simply one of the inheritance of authority on earth. No one should think that he can take it, or keep it, by his own power. It is Allah who grants power and authority to anyone He wills just as He also removes it from anyone He wills.

The Divine Decree and Free Will

Thus everything that happens in the universe is by the power of Allah Almighty and is His real will in His universe. No one can ever prevent or stop it, or even do anything contrary to the real will of Allah in His universe. It is dominant over all and we have no choice.

The things that happen to us by the power of Allah are outside our domain of choice. But neither do we have any freedom of choice in respect of the things that happen to us at the hands of others. If you walk down the road and someone punches you or hits you with a stone or fires a bullet at you, or if someone attacks you when you are at home, all these incidents and other things which happen to you at someone else's hands are outside the circle of your choice. You have no choice when someone attacks you by word or deed, by, for instance, calling you names or hitting or killing you. All this is outside your human choice.

In this way it can be seen that the circle of free choice becomes narrower and narrower until nothing is left except what you do - the things you yourself do or say. You have no choice regarding any of the other incidents in this life. You have no choice in your birth, death, the hours of your sleep, or the things that happen to you from Allah or from others. The only thing left is what you do and even in this narrow circle you only have very limited freedom of choice. Regarding the rest you have no choice at all.

Chapter Four:
Free Will and Responsibility

Our discussion of *Qada'* and *Qadar* has brought us to a specific point, namely that you have no choice except in respect of the things that you do, and even then you do not have an absolute choice, but only a limited one. For not everything you do is of your own will. In fact there is very little that is subject to your will.

Before we proceed, we must first know what an action is. There are words, deeds and actions. Each has a different meaning. Words are the deeds of the tongue whose function is to speak. So all speech comes from the tongue. Deeds are the function of bodily organs which perform them, that is, carry out man's will. Action is agreement between word and deed. So Allah says:

> "O you who believe! why do you say what you do not do? Very hateful is it to Allah that you say what you do not do." (61:2-3)

Accordingly, there are words, deeds, and actions. Man may have power over words but not over action. How? Because action has conditions that are not subject to man's choice. The first of these conditions is time and place, for every action needs a time and a place. We measure time by the events that happen, or in other words, by the actions that take place.

Anything that happens in a person's life requires time, even if it is only a few seconds. In this world, we measure our life by time. This work takes a year and that takes two; this happened one hundred years ago and that happened thousands of years ago; this will happen tomorrow or the day after tomorrow or next year; this man is twenty and that man is seventy or eighty years old.

Thus all the events of life are measured by time, which is controlled by Allah Almighty who created it. We do not control time, rather it controls us. Nobody can stop time; in other words remain a child instead of growing up, or a young man instead of progressing to old age. None of us can bring back time that has passed, bring back something that happened one, two or a few years ago.

Likewise none of us controls future time so as, for instance, to be able to make twenty years pass in a single day. Since we neither own time nor are able to control it, we are also unable to control its events. Consequently, everything we do in relation to time is outside our ability to choose, for we own only the present moment in which we live.

Action - For Whom?

When you say, "I will do something tomorrow," we say that you have said something you cannot guarantee or control, for you might not live till tomorrow to do that thing. And even if you do live till tomorrow, you may be sick and therefore not have the strength or the power to do it. You may become busy with something else, for example one of your children may fall ill or die, so you will not be able to fulfil your intention. The same thing may happen to the person who is to do the thing with you. Suppose you have agreed with someone to meet tomorrow in a certain place, then something happens to that man: an urgent matter or an accident or his death occurs, in that event the meeting and the action will not take place.

Every action needs a time and a place. These are essential conditions on earth and in this life. It is possible that Allah might give you the element of time but not give you the element of place. Suppose you are intending to build a tower in a particular place. In the morning you may go to the place and find out that the government has taken the land for a public utility, or find that somebody

36

claims the land is his and stops you from building, or you may not find the engineer to supervise the project, or the workers to do the work, or you may not find the building materials you need. You do not have control over these things: you do not control the elements of the action. But Allah does control it. Therefore He says:

"Never say about anything, 'I am doing that tomorrow,' without saying 'If Allah wills.' Remember your Lord when you forget, and say, 'Perhaps my Lord will guide me to something closer to right guidance than this.'" (18:23-24)

This means that you must have proper behaviour in regard to what you say and ascribe the action to its true owner, not ascribe it to yourself and say, "I'll do such-and-such." Instead, ascribe it to Allah, for He is the owner of all the real elements of the action. It is He who owns your life, He who keeps you alive until you have done the thing you wanted or ends your life before you can do it. It is He who possesses the power, and then either gives it to you so that you can do it or takes it back from you so that you are unable to do it.

It is He who controls the element of place, and either reserves it for you so that you can do what you want, or else makes the action impossible for you. It is He who has the power to make use of anyone He wills to help you do the thing you want, or else does not make them available, so that you are not able to do it. Since these factors are in the hand of Allah, you must then ascribe the action to its owner and say, *"In sha'a'llah* (If Allah wills)."

Thus the occurrence and completion of the action lie in the power of Allah alone. None of us has the power to do what he wants, except by the will of Allah who gives us the necessary life and energy to perform the action.

The Action and the Decree

Even in the things that are seemingly subjected to your will by Allah, the action is not done except by His permission. The foot will not move a single step unless He gives it the strength to step forward. The hand will not move unless He gives it the power to move. Someone might argue with this. We say to him: "Look into yourself and to your conscious movements and you will know that they are accomplished by the power of Allah. When you are seated and need to stand up, all you do is to want to stand up and Allah gives you the strength to do so. If you claim that this happens by your own will and power, tell us how many muscles you move when you do it? How many muscles stretch or expand making you able to stand up?"

The answer is that most of us do not know. Only those who have studied the muscles and their movements know, and even they stand up spontaneously. If a man were to stand up by an act of his will, he would have to give instructions to certain muscles to shrink and to others to stretch and it would take him a very long time to stand up, for he would have to order each muscle individually.

The same thing happens when a person wants to walk. He does not know anything about the movements that take place inside his body when he walks. If he needs to go faster or to run, many more things happen inside his body: his heart increases its pulse rate so that the body can get the extra oxygen needed for running, his blood circulation becomes faster, his breathing becomes more rapid, and the muscles move in a different way from when he is walking. All of this happens without any personal choice and is accomplished by the power of Allah who gives the body the strength to perform all these movements without any choice at all on the part of man.

Will and Movement

These movements, whether voluntary or involuntary, take place at a tremendous speed, beyond the scope of human choice to order this to happen and that not to. This energising ability is granted by Allah and no one can claim it to be automatic, or that it happens by a human choice. It is just that Allah has placed in you this capacity for movement and given you choice with regard to directing it.

You can direct that latent energy created by Allah in the pursuit of good or evil; you can walk to the mosque or to the pub. May Allah protect us! This walking is not done automatically: it is Allah who gives the energy. What you have done is to direct this capacity to either good or evil.

Your hand can hold a knife to cut something into suitable pieces for your mouth so that you can eat. You can also hold the same knife to murder someone. In both cases, you did not create the capacity in the hand to do this. That capacity is a gift from Allah. All you did was to exploit the capacity given by Allah, in the hand that is created by Allah, to do good or evil.

The tongue may tell the truth or tell a lie; it may say a good or bad word. However, you have no power of your own to make your tongue speak. You can only use that capacity for speech granted by Allah to your tongue to obey or disobey. All the organs of your body may seem to be subject to your choice but they are not. They do not move by your will. They move by the power which Allah has put into them. The only choice you have is whether to do good or evil.

This is the limit of the choice Allah has given you: to use that power for good or evil. This is the boundary of accountability - the Trust man has undertaken. Allah has willed that choice in us. Had He not created us with that choice, we would not have been able to choose; but we do have that choice within the limit of responsibility and in respect of the things Allah has willed that we should enjoy in life out of His divine bounties. We may choose what we like from among foods, drinks and clothes, and so on. We have no choice regarding anything except these things.

Free Will in Pursuing the Way

In this way we have the free will to implement the commands and prohibitions of Allah and this is the arena of accountability on the Day of Judgement, for responsibility entails the laws concerning the commands and prohibitions. It is not lawful for man to make the commands into prohibitions or vice versa. You are contradicting the Law of Allah when you do what He has prohibited and do not do what He has commanded. This is the domain of your choice, for which you will be held accountable in the Hereafter.

Here we come to the real arena of man's freedom of choice in this life, that sphere which Allah Almighty has created in which He has given us full freedom of choice.

Why, then, act contrary to the Law of Allah and do what He has forbidden and not do what He has commanded? This is because Allah has given me free will in this particular area. If He had not made me free to choose, I would not be able to do what He has forbidden. So, you can act contrary to the Law of Allah through the freedom of choice He has given you. Therefore, even here it is only Allah's precedent will to let you choose that has allowed you the ability to make a free choice.

The Meaning of Responsibility

Having understood that, we should know that the meaning of responsibility and human free will entails the exercise of choice in respect of the commands and prohibitions which constitute the basis of accountability in the Hereafter. It may happen that this freedom is confronted by an irresistible power that compels you to do something without your being able to choose. In such a case, we say that you are not responsible or accountable. Thanks to His justice, Allah does not judge you in such instances, for He has curtailed your free will so that you cannot choose with full freedom to do good or evil.

Let us suppose that a man comes and chains me so that I cannot do my prayers. Am I then accountable for not praying or not? Suppose that a man compels me to prostrate to something other than Allah, am I held accountable? The answer is, of course, no, for Allah says:

"Anyone who rejects Allah after having belief, except for someone who is compelled to it but whose heart remains at rest in its belief." (16:106)

Thus compulsion removes accountability, because Allah - glory be to Him! - has given us full freedom of choice in the implementation of His way. He wants us to come to Him with love. That is why He wants us to affirm that love for His Most High Being. So when someone commits a sin by being compelled to do it through no choice of his own, he is not punished; and likewise someone who performs an act of obedience under compulsion and with no freedom of choice is not rewarded for it.

In matters of worship, the quality of love for Allah's sake must be really confirmed. If there is no true love for the sake of Allah in the heart of the believer, and if there is no true recourse to Allah, then the actions of that person will not be accepted. Thus, when a person gives in charity just so that people will say that he is charitable and a man of goodness and piety, then he receives no reward from Allah, for he did not do it out of love for Allah - glory be to Him! - but merely for the sake of fame and glory in this world.

When someone contributes to a charity organisation chaired by a woman whose husband is a man of influence and then expects her husband to do him a worldly favour, he has no reward. He has chosen a worldly benefit and has not given the charity out of love for Allah. When a man performs his prayers so that people will say that he is devout, or performs *hajj* in order to show off, he too has no reward, for he intends to gain repute in this life and his heart is void of love for Allah. Concerning such a situation, the Messenger of Allah, may Allah bless him and grant him peace, said:

"Actions only go by intentions. Everyone gets what they intend. Anyone, therefore, who emigrates to Allah and His Messenger, his emigration is indeed to Allah and His Messenger. But anyone who emigrates to gain something of this world or to marry a woman, his emigration is to that to which he emigrated." (an-Nawawi, *Forty Hadith*)

It is therefore necessary for man to have full freedom to use his intellect and direct the capacity created by Allah towards obedience or sin if he is to be held accountable in the Hereafter. Compelling someone to commit a sin, like adultery, is not accepted. Allah Almighty says:

> "*Do not force your slavegirls to prostitute themselves, if they desire to be virtuous women, out of your desire for this world. If anyone forces them, then, after they have been forced, Allah is Forgiving, Merciful.*" (24:33)

So we can see that even if major sins, such as *kufr* and adultery, are committed under compulsion, there will be no punishment. The action must be done by employing the capacity created for us by Allah through the intellect and the free will to do good or evil. Thus Allah's justice requires that insane people be exempt from being held responsible, for their intellect cannot direct its capacity towards good or evil through the exercise of their own free will. A mad person cannot distinguish between the harmful and the beneficial. It is the same with a child under the age of puberty, for his mind is too immature to understand the correct choice.

Willingly or Unwillingly

Some people may ask how it is that Allah has given man full freedom in the domain of responsibility, i.e. to act or not to act, but has made accountability depend on intention, not upon the outward form of the action? Allah Almighty says about accountability on the Day of Judgement:

> *"On the day when the secrets are tried, he will have no strength, no helper."* (86:9-10)

If this is the situation, and if man has been given choice in this matter, how can we explain Allah's saying:

> *"Everyone in the heavens and the earth prostrates to Allah willingly or unwillingly, as do their shadows in the morning and evening."* (13:15)

We say that this verse means both in this life and the Afterlife. All those in the heavens and on earth had been prostrating themselves to Allah - glory be to Him! - willingly, i.e. by their own choice in this life. Each thing in the universe except men and jinn prostrates itself willingly since it has chosen to be subjugated of its own choice. As for men and jinn, some of them have chosen to prostrate themselves willingly in this life, but in the Afterlife, there will be no choice, for men and jinn will also be constrained. When Allah wills them to prostrate themselves to Him, no one will be able to refuse. If Allah wills them not to be able to prostrate, they will not be able to do it, even unwillingly. This verse testifies to this:

> *"On the day when legs are bared, and they are called to bow themselves, but they cannot, their eyes will be cast down and abasement will overcome them, for they were summoned to bow themselves while they were whole."* (68:42-43)

Then prostration takes place voluntarily in this life, while it is involuntary in the Afterlife because freedom of choice ends at death and all become submitted to Allah - glory be to Him and may He be exalted!

Freedom of Choice and its Removal

Here we must draw attention to an important point. Allah Almighty wanted to call our attention to the fact that the choice given us in this life comes from His power and will. If He wants to take it back, He can, for it is given by Him and by His will. That is why Allah says about Abu Lahab, an uncle of the Prophet, may Allah bless him and grant him peace, and one of the leaders of *kufr* who fought fiercely against the faith of Allah:

> *"Perish the hands of Abu Lahab and perish he! His wealth avails him not, nor what he has earned; he shall roast in a blazing fire, and his wife, the carrier of the firewood, upon her neck a rope of palm-fibre."* (111)

In His Glorious Qur'an, which was sent down to His Messenger, may Allah bless him and grant him peace, which cannot be altered or changed, and whose recitation will endure to the Day of Rising, Allah - glory be to Him! - announces that Abu Lahab will die as a *kafir* and will go to Hellfire. What would have happened if Abu Lahab had gathered the people together and said to them, "Muhammad claims that the Qur'an is revealed from Allah and says that I will die as a *kafir* and go to the Fire. Now I say before you: 'I bear witness that there is no god but Allah and Muhammad is His Prophet' so that you know that nothing is being revealed from heaven to him," he would have said that out of hypocrisy or to show off, so as to destroy the whole *deen*.

But Allah Almighty challenged Abu Lahab to exert his free will. It did not occur to his mind to use that challenge to destroy the *deen* one of whose fiercest opponents he was. Many of those Quraysh leaders who waged war against Islam, such as Abu Sufyan, 'Ikrima, Khalid ibn al-Walid, 'Amr b. al-'As and others later became good believers, except Abu Lahab who remained a *kafir* until he died.

Allah wants us to bear this in mind: He, who has given man a free choice, could, if He wanted, take it away, without giving us any choice. So He took away part of Abu Lahab's choice. He gave him the possibility of ruining the *deen* of Allah, but he was unable to and it did not occur to his mind, for in this point he had no free will.

Thus we can see by definite evidence that Allah is He who has given man the freedom of choice in the realm of responsibility and that if He wills, He can take that choice away partially or completely.

So far we have come to the conclusion that actions come from Allah Almighty. They cannot be accomplished except by His permission and we have no freedom of choice, for He controls all every factor bearing on the action. We have seen that man's freedom of choice lies in his directing that capacity created for him to do good or evil and that Allah has given man full freedom in the domain of responsibility - the divine commands and prohibitions. It is therefore possible for him to do what is prohibited and not do what is commanded and he is held accountable for that. However, even this freedom of choice is subject to the will of Allah. He can withhold it completely or in part as He wills, so that we know it proceeds from Allah and not from man, and therefore that it is Allah who has willed us to have freedom of choice.

Chapter Five:
Except What Allah Wills

We have seen that Allah has granted man free will to use the capacity created by Allah in his body either for obedience or for disobedience. We have stated that Allah has given man full freedom to direct this capacity as he wishes so that he will receive a fair accounting. We find, however, that some people pause at the following verses from the Qur'an:

"We have not sent any Messenger except with the language of his people in order to make things clear to them. Allah leads astray anyone He wills and guides anyone He wills. He is the Mighty, the Wise." (14:4)

And also:

"Thus Allah leads astray anyone He wills and guides anyone He wills, and no one knows the hosts of your Lord except Him." (74:31)

There are many other verses in the Holy Qur'an, some of which will be dealt with in this chapter, that make it clear to us that Allah leads astray anyone He wills and guides anyone He wills. If this is the reality, that the will of Allah guides and leads astray, how then can the Reckoning be fair? Does any of us control anything himself in the face of the will of Allah Almighty?

We say that Allah has absolute power in His universe. All the laws and causes of this universe are Allah's creation. No one can control the will of his Creator. Allah is He who created the laws of this universe and it is He who breaks these laws for His Messengers. He made fire which burns, but made it cool and a means of safety for Ibrahim, peace be upon him. He made the sea, which drowns, split apart for Musa, peace be upon him. By His authority, He gave 'Isa, peace be upon him, the ability to give sight to the blind, heal lepers, and bring the dead to life. Allah gave all these miracles to His Prophets as confirmation that they were conveying the message of Allah. However, His might is not confined to His Prophets. Rather, every day we see His power manifest when a weak person defeats a powerful one, or an oppressed man overcomes a tyrant or an underprivileged human being masters people with great influence.

Unrestrained Power

If each of us reviews his life, he will discover that there was at least one day when he cried out from the depths of his soul, "Our Lord is great" or "Our Lord exists" or "Your Lord defers, but He does not disregard." We do not say this except when we witness an event where divine power manifests itself. Things that happen in the normal way do not make us say this. The strong winning victory over the weak does not make us say, "Our Lord exists," for what has taken place was according to the law of causation we see unfolding every day. The oppressor defeating the oppressed does not make us say, "Your Lord defers, but He does not disregard." We do not witness the display of power except when people are wronged, for the reckoning is postponed to the Day of Judgement except in the case of the oppression of other people. This must be punished by Allah in this life in order to keep the balance, and so that people know that wrongdoing brings retribution in this life as well as in the life to come.

The Messenger of Allah, may Allah bless him and grant him peace, said:

> "Beware the supplication of the wronged. There is no veil between it and Allah. Allah raises it above the clouds

and says, 'By My Might and Majesty, I will help you, even
if it is after a time.''

The Meaning of Guidance

Allah's justice has demanded that man be granted freedom of
choice in respect of the way he follows. How, in the face of this
freedom, is it then possible to say that Allah guides and leads
astray anyone He wills? Before dealing with this point, we have to
understand the meaning of guidance.

Guidance means showing someone the way. When someone
asks you about a certain route, you tell him to go in such-and-such
direction, then right or left, and he will find the place he is looking
for. You have guided him to it. At the same time, guidance is also
used to mean helping someone on his way. When a person asks
about the way that leads to a specific place, you tell him there are
two ways leading in that direction and recommend one of them
because it is safe whereas the other is dangerous owing to high-
waymen. You not only told him the way, but you also helped him
to take the safe way.

The first guidance showing the way comes from Allah for
every act of worship. The Prophets came to guide mankind to the
Straight Path. They conveyed their messages to their peoples in
order to guide them to the Straight Way of Allah and show them
the way that pleases or displeases Him. This constitutes perfect
guidance to all mankind. After the final message of Muhammad,
may Allah bless him and grant him peace, the Muslims were given
the task of guiding people to the way of Islam, i.e. telling and
showing them its teachings. If we do not do this, we will be held
accountable for it.

If a man is lives alone in a faraway cave and the message has
never reached him, then he will not be held accountable on the
Day of Judgement. The task of conveying the Message of Allah is
something that is still going on. To prove it, we can cite the example of the orientalists who have been doing their best to attack the

Islamic *Deen*. They have been told and they know full well that there is a *deen* and a way to Allah called Islam. There are others who know that the Islamic *deen* and way exist, but they do not care to find out or read anything about it or even to listen to people who might tell them something about its rules. These will be held accountable, for when a person, in his daily life, hears about anything of interest to him, he should ask and read about it.

If someone wishes to get a particular job, he will make sure he makes himself properly qualified for it. He will enrol in the appropriate college to gain qualification for that job and will even pursue extra studies to increase his knowledge about it. When a man wants to buy something, he will investigate all the available makes in the market and compare their prices and qualities in order to buy the cheapest and the best. This even applies to luxuries such as tourism. When someone wants to visit a particular country, he will read about it in order to know what places to see and where he should stay, etc. If this is the concern we show in matters connected with our day to day existence, is it not more important to show far more concern in the matter of Allah's *deen*, undoubtedly the most important matter in our life?

However many of us are more interested in the trivial concerns of this life. When they hear about Allah's *deen,* which guides to the Straight Path and leads man to eternal bliss or, if not followed, to eternal punishment, they do not care, and yet they will be held to account for that.

Thus guidance means showing the way to Allah so that people come to know the *deen* of Allah, and worship and obey all His commands. However, there is another meaning, which is the help and support given by Allah to His believing servants. When a person becomes a believer, Allah gives him support and more guidance. To this effect Allah says:

"But those who are rightly guided, He increases them in guidance, and gives them their fear of Him." (47:17)

Then you read Allah's words addressed to His Prophet Muhammad, may Allah bless him and grant him peace:

*"You cannot guide those you love, rather Allah guides
those He wills."* (28:56)

and further:

"You most certainly guide to a straight path." (42:52)

We find in these *ayats* that Allah - glory be to Him! - ascribes
guidance to the Prophet, may Allah bless him and grant him peace,
in one and denies it to him in the other. If you ask how it was possible for the Prophet, may Allah bless him and grant him peace, to
guide to the Straight Path when he was unable to guide those he
loved, we say this shows that the meanings of the Holy Qur'an are
not fully understood by you. The guidance ascribed by Allah to
His Prophet, may Allah bless him and grant him peace, is the guidance of direction, since the Prophet directed people to the way of
belief, the way to obedience, and showed them what displeases
Allah and incurs His punishment. The other kind of guidance,
which Allah did not ascribe to His Prophet, may Allah bless him
and grant him peace, is the guidance of support, because it is Allah
who gives increased guidance to all those who follow the way of
guidance, grants them help and support, and makes the *deen* dear
to them. Allah Almighty says:

*"But Allah has endeared belief to you, making it pleas-
ing to your hearts, and He has made unbelief and ungod-
liness and disobedience detestable to you. Those - they are
the right-guided."* (49:7)

Actual and Legal Will

Allah - glory be to Him! - has an actual will in His universe,
and no one can counter it, for it is effective. He also has a legal
will in His universe, and this concerns what He has enjoined on
people in His *deen*. This divine legal will gives man freedom of

choice to obey or disobey, for Allah has given man the freedom to obey and the freedom to disobey. It is this legal will of do's and don'ts which humans oppose. As for the actual will concerning the events which take place in Allah's universe, no one can oppose them. Just read this verse:

"As for Thamud, We guided them, but they preferred blindness to guidance." (41:17)

This means that Allah - glory be to Him! - guided Thamud to the path of guidance and showed it to them, but they preferred to disobey and leave obedience aside. Every human being can do that through the will of Allah who created man with the freedom of choice either to carry out the commands of Allah or to follow the path of disobedience.

Out of His mercy, Allah - glory be to Him! - has told us what will happen if we follow the path of guidance or the path of mis-guidance. Out of His mercy, He has placed the keys to both Paradise and the Fire in our hands. So whoever wants to follow the way of Paradise must believe in Allah, and whoever follows the way to the Fire will travel the path of disobedience of Allah.

Allah Almighty has shown us what He will do with those who follow the way of belief and with those who follow the way of dis-obedience and rejection. Those who follow the way of belief and find the fulfilment of Allah's promise, will realise that Allah's will has been achieved. Those who follow the path of disobedience and rejection and find the fulfilment of Allah's threat, will also realise that Allah's will has been achieved. Neither the believer nor the unbeliever can revolt against the will of Allah. Here accountability is fair in both cases, since man has chosen with his own free will the way of belief or disobedience. And Allah has shown him what will happen to him if he follows either way.

No Punishment without a Text

Allah - glory be to Him! - does not punish for any sin unless it has been forbidden by Him first. Many societies have extracted from this the legal principle: No punishment without a text. There must be a preceding text to establish a particular action as a crime. After the prohibiting text has been made known, anyone who commits the prohibited act becomes a criminal deserving punishment. Allah Almighty has shown what will happen to those who follow the way of belief. He says:

> *"But those who are rightly guided, He increases them in guidance, and gives them their fear of Him."* (47:17)

And He says:

> *"But Allah has endeared belief to you, making it pleasing to your hearts, and He has made unbelief and ungodliness and disobedience detestable to you. Those - they are the right-guided."* (49:7)

He also says:

> *"Anyone who comes with a good action will have ten like it."* (6:160)

And Allah Almighty further says:

> *"The likeness of those who spend their wealth in the way of Allah is that of a grain which produces seven ears, in each ear a hundred grains. Allah gives exponential increase to anyone He wills. Allah is Boundless, All-Knowing."* (2:261)

There are many other verses which indicate the good that will happen to man if he travels the path of belief. Allah has made it clear how He will help the believer, and reward and support him in this worldly life. Here, we are not dealing with the Hereafter, for that is another subject. In a *hadith qudsi*, Allah says:

"I fulfil My slave's expectation of Me, and I am with him when he remembers Me. If he remembers Me in himself, I remember him in Myself; and if he remembers Me in a gathering, I remember him before a gathering far better than them. If he draws nearer to Me by a handbreadth, I draw nearer to him by an arm's length; and if he draws nearer to Me by an arm's length, I draw nearer to him by a fathom. If he comes to Me walking, I go to him running."

All these blessings come from Allah to help us towards belief and are mentioned and indicated by Him to specify the way. If we follow the way of belief, all these blessings will come to us. It is important for us to take the first step, then every possible support and aid will follow from Allah Almighty. If we take the first step towards belief, choose the way of belief, we will enjoy all these blessings by the will of Allah. But if we choose the way of disbelief and leave the way of belief - may Allah protect us! - what will happen to us? Allah Almighty says:

"Anyone who takes Shaytan as a protector instead of Allah, has clearly lost completely." (4:119)

He says:

"Recite to them the tale of him to whom We gave Our signs, and who then cast them aside and followed Shaytan. He was one of those lured into misguidance." (7:175)

He says:

"Whoever shuts his eyes to the remembrance of the Merciful, We consign a shaytan to him and he becomes his intimate." (43:36)

54

He says:

> *"We have made the shaytans the friends of those who do
> not believe."* (7:27)

He says:

> *"Shall I inform you of the one on whom the shaytans
> come down? They come down on every evil liar."*
> (26:221-2)

And many other verses in the Holy Qur'an make it clear that
Allah forsakes those who do not believe. He will leave them for
the shaytans to seduce and tempt to do falsehood and lead into disobedience, so that they commit more sins and acts of disobedience
and then punishment becomes their due. Allah seals up their hearts
so that disbelief will never leave them. They may themselves
become human shaytans - may Allah protect us! - until they end
up with what He has prepared for the unbelievers who have gone
astray.

When you believe, you join your will to belief, and Allah will
give you all that He has promised the believers. But when you join
your will to disbelief, you will join the shaytans. In neither situation are you independent of the will of Allah, whether you take the
way of belief or disbelief.

Those Not Guided by Allah

Allah has shown us those who are not covered by His will of
guidance. He says:

> *"Allah does not guide rejecting people."* (2:261)

And He says:

"Allah does not guide wrongdoing people." (2:258)

And He says:

"Allah does not guide people who are wantonly deviant." (9:24)

And He says:

"Allah does not guide anyone who is an ungrateful liar." (39:3)

And He says:

"Allah does not guide anyone who is a profligate persistent liar." (40:28)

Thus Allah shows us who are deprived of His guidance. If someone is a rejecter, wrongdoer, a deviant, an ungrateful liar, or a profligate persistent liar, Allah will not guide them. Guidance here means helping towards belief and its increase. Allah makes this clear to us so that we may keep away from these things and abstain from doing them in order to conform with His wishes and guidance.

In any event, however, you remain within the will of Allah and cannot leave it. If you choose to avoid rejection, wrongdoing and deviance, you come under the will of guidance. But if you choose the way of rejection and wrongdoing, you fall under His will that there be no guidance for you. So in neither of these situations are you outside His will, for nothing can happen to you except what Allah wills for you. We cannot escape Allah's will, no matter what way we choose.

This is the truth which you must know, so that you do not think when you believe or disbelieve that you have escaped His will. What happens is that you have obeyed or disobeyed Allah's legal will, but you do not and will not escape His will.

We have now established that all that takes place comes from the will of Allah; that Allah has created His directive guidance for all mankind - believers and unbelievers - as well as supportive guidance only for the believers to increase their guidance; and that Allah has manifested His will to those who believe and those who do not believe in Him. We have also demonstrated how He increases the belief and guidance of the believer, and how He leaves the unbeliever for shaytans to tempt him to disobedience and inveigle him to disobey, until his heart becomes sealed up, unable to escape from disbelief.

When you choose belief or disbelief, whatever happens to you takes place by the will of Allah, either by increasing your guidance or by causing you to follow Shaytan. In either case, you are subject to the will of Allah. If you obey the legal will of Allah in His universe, you are subject to His will; and if you disobey, you are still subject to His will.

Chapter Six:
Allah Encompasses All Things

We have spoken of the believers and unbelievers and shown how neither of them transcend the divine will. What they do is either obey or oppose Allah's legal will in existence. However, certain arguments which have been forward by unbelievers have made it necessary to reply to some points. Man has always been contentious, trying to find a way to escape from Allah's punishment. He claims that this punishment comes from Allah's will, and that therefore he has no choice about it anyway.

To this we say, "Yes, it is from the will of Allah, but it is you who choose the way to His will, so that you either enter into His mercy and His bliss, or choose the way to His wrath and His punishment. The key is in your own hands. You believe and Allah increases your belief. You stand at night offering your prayers and Allah elevates your station. You recite the Qur'an and Allah increases your reward. You do good and Allah gives you a high rank. When you turn aside from all this, Allah will increase you in deviation from obedience to Him and leave you to Shaytan."

In argument some people cite the noble verse of the Qur'an where Allah says:

"We have created many men and jinn for Jahannam. They have hearts they do not understand with. They have eyes they do not see with. They have ears they do not hear with. Such people are like cattle. No, they are even further astray! Those are the heedless ones." (7:179)

Those who want to argue vainly say: "Since Allah has created these for Hellfire and given them hearts that cannot understand, eyes that do not see and ears that do not hear, what is the crime that causes them to be punished in Hellfire?"

We say to such people, "You have not understood the meaning of this verse. Allah has created for those people hearts that understand, but they do not use them to understand with. He has created for them eyes that can see, but it is they who do not choose to see with them. He also created for them ears, but they do not use them to hear with.

Take their hearts, for example, which is where faith has its place: they reject sound logical argument even when it is clearly and lucidly presented to them. For instance, they are the kind of people alluded to in the following verse:

"When they say, 'O Allah! If this is really the Truth from You, rain down on us stones from heaven or bring upon us a painful punishment.'" (8:32)

Could this be said by people who truly use their hearts to understand with? Would it not be more reasonable to say, "If this is really the truth from Allah, O Lord guide us to it!"? Regarding this particular point, they have used a twisted logic and prefer to be punished rather than to believe the truth. However, in worldly affairs such as trade, people like these make sound decisions to increase their fortune, and so on. They prepare themselves for caravans and deal with dirhams and dinars in a most astute way. The speakers in this verse were in fact the leaders of Quraysh and the richest of the Arabs. When the true religion came, they refused to use sound understanding or sound reasoning. They started talking like those who have no hearts that can understand or know. Allah did not create them with hearts that did not understand. He created them with sound hearts, but they refused to understand or to use their hearts correctly. They knew that the Message of Muhammad, may Allah bless him and grant him peace, was the Truth. However, out of pure negligence, they sought punishment rather than believe in it.

The Eye Can See . . . But . . .

As for the heedless people's eyes, we find that Allah has given them eyes which can see, but they do not use that capacity. Musa was sent to the people of Pharaoh with many signs which they witnessed with their own eyes. Concerning this, Allah says:

> *"So We sent down upon them the flood, and locusts and lice and frogs and blood, signs clear and distinct, but they were arrogant and were an evil-doing people."* (7:133)

All these signs sent by Allah to Pharaoh's people could easily be seen: the flood that inundated the land was clear to everyone; the locusts that devoured the plants were seen by all; the lice and the frogs were found in their food; and there was the water which turned into blood whenever they tried to drink. Did not all of them see all these signs? Yes, but although they saw them, they did not believe them, just as if their eyes could not see. The purpose of seeing is to know the thing seen, to identify and believe what you see.

These people saw but did not believe, and so they are the same as those who do not see at all. The Prophet, may Allah bless him and grant him peace, was asked by the unbelievers to split the moon as a sign to prove that he had indeed come with the truth from his Lord. When Allah responded to His Prophet, may Allah bless him and grant him peace, and the moon was split, did they believe what they saw? No, they said, "Muhammad has bewitched our eyes." They were just like people who cannot see, for they saw but denied what they saw.

As for their ears that do not hear, did not the Qur'an report what the unbelievers of Quraysh said?

> *"Those who reject say, 'Do not listen to this Qur'an but rather make a nonsense of it, so that it may be that you will triumph.'"* (41:26)

61

Their ears are healthy and can hear, but they do not use them to listen to the words of Allah, and they also ask other people not to listen, in spite of the fact that they should have listened and understood. Did they not accuse the Messenger, may Allah bless him and grant him peace, of being a poet, a soothsayer and insane? Was that compatible with the deeds and sayings of the Prophet, may Allah bless him and grant him peace?

Did he ever utter a single line of poetry before he took on the message so that they could call him a poet? Did he practise magic before the message so that they could justifiably term him a magician? Did they hear anything from the Prophet, may Allah bless him and grant him peace, except for the best words in all he said, and witness anything but the best deeds in all he did? They used to call him "the Trustworthy" and bear witness that he used to have immense character. Yet when he brought the Message, they accused him of madness.

Were their unfounded accusations against the Prophet, may Allah bless him and grant him peace, compatible with what they saw, heard, grasped and understood about the Prophet, may Allah bless him and grant him peace, the noblest of all humanity? Of course not, but their reasoning capabilities worked in a natural way before Muhammad, may Allah bless him and grant him peace, was sent with the Message. That is why they called him "the Trustworthy, a person with immense character" and someone who never lied or betrayed any trust.

But after the Message was given to the Prophet, may Allah bless him and grant him peace, they did not use their intellects, eyes or ears. They started talking out of passion and caprice, exactly like those who do not understand, see or hear.

Therefore, to say that Allah did not create for them hearts to understand, eyes to see or ears to hear is simply not true. It was they who did not employ those senses because they did not want to believe. They just did not use them. Had they used those senses in the proper way, they would have believed.

Allah's Knowledge Encompasses Everything

Allah says:

"We have created many men and jinn for Jahannam."

From the hour of their creation, those referred to have been condemned by Allah Almighty to be among the people of Hellfire, though they had not yet done anything. We say that this is part of Allah's comprehensive knowledge of His universe. His knowledge is infinite. He knew from the moment of their creation that they were going to be among the dwellers of Hellfire. How can people say this is strange, when it is clear that His knowledge encompasses everything in this world and the next? Did not Nuh, peace be upon him, say this to Allah?

"And Nuh said, 'My Lord, do not leave even one of the unbelievers on the earth. Surely, if You leave them, they will lead Your servants astray, and will beget none but unbelieving libertines." (71:26-7)

Who told Nuh that these unbelievers would only breed unbelieving libertines? He judged merely from the actions he saw before him while preaching the Message to his people, having lived for nine hundred and fifty years among them. Did not Iblis say the following?

"(Iblis) said 'By Your might, I will mislead all of them except for Your chosen slaves among them.'" (38:81-2)

Who told Iblis that he was going to tempt every insincere servant of Allah? Allah explains this to us when He says:

"Iblis was quite correct in his assessment of them, and so they followed him, with the exception of a group of believers." (34:20)

Iblis was not guessing when he said this, for he sensed then that Adam and Eve were open to temptation.

Now, we move to the ordinary man. If you see your child not studying and neglecting his lessons, you will tell him that he will not pass this year. Then he really does not pass. Did you know the unseen, or did you simply take stock of the situation and reach a logical conclusion? A teacher tells his class of twenty pupils that only ten will pass, and that is exactly what happens. Did he know the future or was he simply judging according to the standard of the pupils?

If this can happen among Allah's creatures, with their limited knowledge and weak powers, do you consider it too much for Allah Almighty, the Most Knowledgeable Creator, to know for certain that a number of His creatures will finally end up in Hellfire? If His creatures can make accurate assessments, can the knowledge of Allah Almighty not reach accurate conclusions? Of course it can and He knows for certain. The Qur'an testifies to this when He says:

"Does He not know, who created? And He is the All-Subtle, the All-Aware." (67:14)

Allah's awareness is far beyond our capabilities and our knowledge and it is easy for Him to know the destiny of His creatures. Some people, however, hesitate at this noble saying of the Prophet:

"A man can do the actions of someone destined for the Garden until there is only an armspan between him and it, and then what is written will overtake him and he will do the actions of someone destined for the Fire and enter it."

How can the reckoning be a fair one when someone behaves like the people of Paradise until he is very close to it, and then he is overtaken by what has already been written for him so that he becomes one of the people of Hellfire? And conversely how can someone behave like the people of Hellfire and then be overtaken by what has already been written for him so that he becomes one of the people of Paradise? If what is "written" is inescapable, then being admitted to Paradise or Hellfire is decreed whatever my deeds are, because the "written" has changed the result of my actions. These assertions are frequently repeated, especially by those who have transgressed against themselves and who want to put the blame for their sins on others or who want to say this is "written" and they cannot change it. That is exactly like the unbelievers, as the Qur'an explains:

> *"Those who associate others with Allah will say, 'If Allah had willed we would not have associated others with Him, and nor would our fathers; nor would we have made anything unlawful.'"* (6:148)

By this argument the unbelievers want to put the blame for associating other gods with Allah on the will of Allah - glory be to Him! We have already made it clear that neither believers nor unbelievers transcend the will of Allah. Those who believe enter the will of belief, and Allah supports them by more guidance and endears belief to them; their final destination is Paradise. Those who disbelieve and associate others with Allah - may Allah protect us! - have entered the will of disbelief and Allah does not grant them support or guidance but leaves them for shaytans to seduce them.

A Warning Against Shaytan

To return to the saying of the Prophet, may Allah bless him and grant him peace: he wanted to warn us against the whisperings of Shaytan and our passions, and to open for us the doors of hope forever, so that the believer would be careful and the disobedient would wait for Allah's forgiveness and hope for repentance. He made it clear in the *hadith* that a man may do the good deeds to make him one of the people of Paradise, but that Shaytan concentrates on tempting the believers and never leaves them alone. As Allah tells us, Shaytan does his best to entice the believers:

"I will sit in ambush for them on your Straight Path."
(7:16)

Shaytan does not concentrate his efforts on places that sell alcoholic drinks, pleasure places and brothels, for those people have already been seduced and they need no more temptation. Their appetites and desires are in agreement, and they have become agents of Satan, who does not need to expend any more effort on them. He concentrates all his efforts on those who are devoted to their prayers, coming at them from all directions, tempting them with forbidden money. When he finds resistance to that, he entices them with adultery by telling how pretty and beautiful unlawful women are! If he does not succeed in these attempts, Satan tries to beguile them into bribery, gambling, telling lies or drinking.

Thus Satan goes on enticing the believer into error and disobedience until he commits it. If he fails here, Shaytan still does not give up, for he comes during the prayer to whisper, for instance, to the worshipper that his ablution was not good so that he does *wudu'* several times. The more he does his ablution, the more Shaytan tells him that this not accepted. When he performs his prayer, Shaytan whispers to him that his prayer is not accepted or complete. He continues whispering to him concerning his duties until matters of worship become too difficult for him, in spite of the fact that religion has been made very easy.

The objective of Shaytan is to make worship too difficult for the believer so that he hates it, or make him lose hope of his worship being accepted by Allah Almighty so that he abandons it.

The Messenger of Allah, may Allah bless him and grant him peace, wants to draw our attention to the means of access that Shaytan has to man so that we know them. He wants us to know that Shaytan will never leave us alone right up to our last breath. He will never give up, but will continue whispering, saying, for example, that your worship is more than sufficient and you are sure to enter Paradise. He goes on repeating that until you become falsely convinced by his logic. Then you begin by doing fewer acts of obedience and prayers, and then he tempts you to disobedience until your feet slip one after the other. The result is the road to disobedience, and what is written will overtake you, that which is decreed for the disobedient and those who have left Allah's path, so they are finally deprived of His support or guidance.

Likewise those who commit sins must be aware that the door of repentance is wide open before them as long as they live, and will remain so until the pangs of death arrive. Therefore, they must hasten to repentance. When they hasten to it and perform the good deeds of the people of Paradise, then they conform with the will of guidance and Allah will help them by guiding them, endearing belief to them and making it beautiful in their hearts, changing their evil deeds into good deeds, and thus they become among the people of Paradise.

Thus we see that the *hadith* does not mean that those who do good deeds will enter Hellfire.

Witnesses against Ourselves

Then we come to a question frequently repeated by those who want to cause doubts about the justice of Allah, and who want to make people despair and abandon their worship. They ask, if it is within the knowledge of Allah that they are among the people of Paradise or Hellfire - may Allah protect us! - whether that is not enough, so that there is no need to do anything.

We say to those people that this life is the place where man does have a choice, and there is a great difference between words and deeds. A man may say many things, but then not do them when the right time comes. A soldier before a battle may say, "I will kill twenty of the enemy soldiers when the battle begins," but when the fight actually begins, he may be the first to flee the battlefield. Someone else may tell you, "I will give you a thousand pounds if you do such-and-such," but when you do it, he becomes a miser and does not give you anything.

Allah - glory be to Him! - calls our attention to this fact. He says in His Mighty Qur'an:

"When a Book does come to them from Allah, confirming what is with them - and they had previously been praying for victory against those who reject - when what they recognise does come to them, they reject it. The curse of Allah is on those who reject." (2:89)

This concerns the Jews who used to say to the unbelievers of Madina that the time for a new Prophet had come. They said, "We will believe in him and follow him and we will kill you with him, the same as 'Ad and Iram." When the Prophet, may Allah bless him and grant him peace, was sent, the Jews were the first to disbelieve in him, wage war against him, and plot to kill him. The people of Pharaoh asked Musa, peace be upon him, to remove the punishment from them, and they promised to believe in him. When Allah answered the prayer of Musa, they did not believe. To this effect Allah says:

"But each time We removed the plague from them, up until a fixed term which they completed, they broke their word." (7:135)

The Glorious Qur'an is full of verses that show us how the unbelievers, the hypocrites, and others say or promise many things, but when the time comes to fulfil their promise, they break it.

Therefore, there is a big difference between words and deeds. This is in order that no man can come to argue on the Day of Rising and say, "Lord! if you had asked me to believe, I would have done so. If you had sent a messenger, we would have followed him, and if you had asked me to do good deeds, I would have done them."

Man must undergo a practical test so that he will have to testify against himself on the Day of Judgement. He will not be able to say, "Lord, if only you had guided me, I would have been guided," for guidance came to him and he did not follow it. He will not be able to say, "Lord! If You had only sent me a messenger, I would certainly have been the first to follow him," for Allah has already sent the Messenger and he was the first to fight him. Thus, on the Day of Judgement, man will become a witness against himself and will not have any argument at the time of his accounting, for he underwent a practical test and failed. Allah Almighty says:

"Read your book! Today your own self is reckoner enough against you!" (17:14)

This test of faith does not take place in this worldly life because Allah does not know or wants to know more: Allah has complete knowledge of all things. It takes place so that people may testify against their own selves, exactly in the same way as we hold an exam for university students. The university does not hold that exam to learn from the students who are taught there, but they do it so that every student will be a witness regarding himself. If a student comes and says, "I'm excellent," they show him his answer sheet so that he can see he has failed, and he cannot argue.

We have now seen that those described by Allah in the Holy Qur'an, those who do not use their hearts to understand, those who do not use their eyes to see, and those who do not use their ears to hear, are the people who stop using their senses correctly and do not use them for the purpose Allah has created them for. We have also discovered that man must beware of the whisperings of Shaytan, for if he follows them it will transfer him from the will of belief to the will of disbelief. However, in neither case does he transcend the will of Allah. We know also that this worldly life is a test and a trial for us so that we will be witnesses against ourselves and have no argument on the Day of Judgement, for the knowledge of Allah encompasses everything.

A Supplication

O Lord! Guide Your servants to the path of guidance and success. Open for them Your gates of mercy, so that they have Your support in the path. Open for them the doors of Your forgiveness, so that their sins are forgiven. And open for them the gates of repentance so that they can enter Paradise, for You are the All-Hearing, the All-Knowing!

Shaykh Muhammad Mitwalli al-Sha'rawi

New Publications

An Nawawi's Forty Hadith

Imam an Nawawi

The Compiler of this short book of Hadith (the sayings of the Prophet Muhammad) was the Imam an Nawawi. Born in 1233 A.D in the Syrian village of Nawa, south of Damascus, he enjoyed during his lifetime a high reputation as a jurists and scholar of Hadith. Having lived a frugal life dedicated to scholarship, an-Nawawi died at his birthplace in the year 1277.

The present selection is generally regarded as the most popular anthology and the best introduction to the study of the Prophet's sayings which, together with the Holy Qur'an, contain the essential teaching of Islam.

ISBN: 978-1-870 582773 | 127 Pages [paperback] | £4.95

Forty Hadith Qudsi

Imam an Nawawi

Hadith Qudsi (Sacred Hadith) are those sayings of the Prophet Muhammad divinely communicated to him, though the actual wording need not necessarily be that of the Almighty.

The present collection has been compiled from all the available books of Hadith.

The forty chosen are all well authenticated and present many of the doctrinal, devotional and ethical elements of Islam. A scholarly introduction deals fully with the subject and shows the way in which Sacred Hadith differ from the Holy Qur'an and Prophetic Hadith.

The selection and translations have been made by two scholars whose previous translation on an-Nawawi's forty Hadith gained wide approval for its accuracy and readability. The present book, a companion volume to an- Nawawi's forty Hadith, has been printed in similar format, with the original Arabic text given alongside the English translation.

ISBN: 978-1-870 582773 | 127 Pages [paperback] | £4.95

Four Imams

Muhammed Abu Zahra

This volume contains the English translation of the four books describing and analysing the life and work of the Imams who founded the four canonical schools of Sunni Islamic law. These men are among Islam's greatest spiritual and intellectual figures. All four books were written in Arabic by the Egyptian scholar Muhammed Abu Zahra, who succeeded admirably in producing a detailed picture and analysis of the four madhabs and their founders, including their legal methodology and conclusions. Today, largely because of ignorance or misunderstanding, millions of Muslims are deprived of the benefits of adherence to a particular madhab. There is also a great deal of futile disagreement amongst the believers. In making Sheikh Abu Zahra's major study available in English for the first time, Dar Al Taqwa hopes and intends that it will help the process of healing the rifts and uniting the Muslim Ummah on the basis of mutual respect and understanding. The Four Imams is a stimulating and enriching read for anyone interested in deepening their knowledge of Islam.

ISBN: 978-1-870 582414 | 518 Pages [hardback] | £30.00

Virtue and Vice
Shaykh Muhammad Mitwalli ash-Sha'rawi

Before every human being lie two possible paths he or she can follow: the path of divine guidance and the path of disobedience to Allah. Allah made these two paths clear and then allowed us freely to choose either obedience to Him and His Mercy or, alternatively, disobedience to Him and His punishment. Allah - blessed and exalted is He! - only gave us this choice for a limited period in our life in this world. He has not given is any choice regarding any of the events of this world, He only gave us a choice with respect to the path we may take: that of obedience or disobedience.

In this book Shaykh Muhammad Mitwalli ash-Sha'rawi deals with obedience and disobedience, virtue and vice; and it shows these two paths, one of which leads to paradise and the other to punishment by Allah in Hellfire. He first deals with aspects of virtue in one's dealings with others and with Allah's creatures, and then obeying Allah's commands and then with aspects of vice in one's dealings and in one's character. Shaykh ash-Sha'rawi discusses with his usual eloquence the theoretical and practical aspects of both paths.

ISBN: 978-1-870582-57-5 | 77 Pages [paperback] | £6.95

The Sunna Of the Prophet
The People of Fiqh versus the People of Hadith
Muhammad Al-Ghazzali

Shaykh Muhammad Al Ghazzali was one of the most influential Islamic scholars of the twentieth century. Born in Buhayra, Egypt in 1223/1917, he eventually entered the Faculty of Usul ad-Din in the University of Al Azhar. In the course of his life, he was imam and lecturer at al-Maktaba al-Khadra in Cairo, a member of the Muslim Brotherhood and close associate of Hasan al-Banna, Undersecretary for Islamic Da'wa in the Egyptian Ministry of Awqaf, and held numerous other posts and teaching positions. He published over sixty books. He died in 1416/1996.

Having published the abridged English translation of Shaykh Muhammad al-Ghazali's seminal Qur'anic commentary under the title Journey through the Qur'an, Dar al-Taqwa have followed it with the translation of a second important work by the shaykh about the nature of the Prophetic Sunna.

This is greatly needed in the present situation when there is so much misinformation about Islam in the media, often aided and abetted by well meaning but sometimes misguided Muslims. Using many examples and his own compendious knowledge, Shaykh Muhammad shows how many hadiths have been misunderstood and misused to paint a distorted picture of Islam. With great courtesy and skill he points out the flaws in the positions adopted by extremists at both ends of the spectrum and allows the true picture of the balance and wisdom which in reality make up the Muhammadan Sunna to emerge.

ISBN: 978-1-870582-51-3 | 162 Pages [paperback] | £13.95

Miracles of the Qur'an
Shaykh Muhammad ash-Sha'rawi

For Muslims, the Holy Qur'an is an inexhaustible and hauntingly beautiful source of guidance, consolation and enlightenment.

Above all, it is the very word of God as revealed to the Prophet Muhammed Salallahu Alayhi Wa Salaam and protected for all time against falsification. Muslims' absolute certainty on this point is often difficult for others to comprehend, however majestic and eloquent the text, even in translation. Sheikh ash Sha'rawi, a distinguished contemporary scholar from Egypt, has written a book designed to be read by Muslims and non Muslims alike. In plain and wholly logical language, Ash Sha'rawi presents objective and well documented evidence of the miraculous nature of the Qur'an.

The Miracles of The Qur'an, now presented in a fluent English translation, is divided into three parts. Part one discusses the nature of miracles and examines those linguistic and rhetorical characteristics of teh Holy Qur'an which Muslims believe - and history has shown to be inimitable by man. In parts two and three the author demonstrates, by profound analysis of numerous passages from the text, that the Qur'an contains irrefutable proof of its direct revelation from Allah, the Omniscient Creator.

This authoritative and highly readable book is essential reading for anyone concerned in understanding the nature of the Holy Scripture of Islam.

ISBN: 978-1-870582-01-8 | 275 Pages [paperback] | £17.95

God Revisited
Nasim Butt

Issues of Belief and Identity in the 21st Century

Is there a God? How can we know the answer? If God exists, what can we know about God? These questions are central to the philosophy of religion, but are of concern to all thinking people. In God Revisited, Nasim Butt tackles the issues, looking at the classical arguments for the existence of God and examining the contemporary challenges to them from sociologists and psychologists as well as philosophers.

The author also examines the nature and the meaning of individuals' religious experiences, and the relation between personal faith and religious pluralism. As a Muslim, Dr Butt evaluates alternative viewpoints on the above issues in terms both of their general validity and (mindful of the need for Muslims to gain a stronger appreciation of the logical basis of religious faith) with reference to an Islamic worldview. All philosophical writing reflects the author's own commitments. Hence completely neutrality is not possible; but that does not preclude a genuine striving for critical honesty. The breadth of viewpoint combined with intellectual insight makes God Revisited a valuable source for readers of all faiths.

Born in 1961 in Pakistan, Dr Nasim Butt was raised in England. He holds a B.Sc., M.Sc and Ph.D. in the history of science from the University of London, as well as an M.B.A in educational management and the National Professional Qualification for Leadership.

Formerly Principal of Brondesbury Boys' College in Northwest London, Dr Butt is a qualified Ofsted inspector who assesses both state and public schools. His specialized interests include the philosophy of science and of religion.

ISBN: 978-1-870582-47-6 | 118 Pages [paperback] | £9.95

New Publications 2010

Title	Price	Quantity
An Nawawi's Forty Hadith	£4.95	
Forty Hadith Qudsi	£4.95	
Four Imams	£30.00	
Virtue and Vice	£6.95	
The Sunnah Of the Prophet	£13.95	
Miracles of the Qur'an	£17.95	
God Revisited	£9.95	

Trade order discounts available for retailers
Package and Postage not included
Please Enquire

Dar Al Taqwa will have more new publications to follow in the coming months.
Our Publications range from different subjects and sciences, including:

Qur'anic Tafseer, Fiqh, Hadith, The Prophet (Peace be upon him) and more

Please phone or email your orders to:

020 7935 6385
Daraltaqwa@mail.com

Our Address:

7A Melcombe Street
Baker Street
London
NW1 6AE